The Tamilian Antiquary

VOL. I. NO. 10

THE ORIGIN OF THE TAMIL VELLALAS

The Tamilian Antiquary

VOL. I. NO. 10

THE ORIGIN OF THE TAMIL VELLALAS

V.J. Thamby Pillai

Editor:
Pandit D. Savariroran

GYAN

Published by

GYAN

Gyan Publishing House
5, Ansari Road
Daryaganj, New Delhi-110002
Phone: 011-47034999, 9811692060
E-mail: books@gyanbooks.com

Distribution Network
gyanbooks.com
India, USA, Canada, UK, Australia, France

ISBN : 978-81-212-6579-9 (PB)
First Published, 1912

2nd Impression 2022

Printed at: Gyan Press, Delhi.

THE ORIGIN OF THE TAMIL VELLALAS
Author: V.J. Thamby Pillai

THE TAMILIAN ANTIQUARY
EDITOR
PANDIT D. SAVARIROYAN

VOL. I, NO.1-10; VOL. II, NO.1-2

VOL. I, NO.10

THE ORIGIN OF THE TAMIL VELLALAS

V. J. THAMBY PILLAI

ASIAN EDUCATIONAL SERVICES
NEW DELHI ★ CHENNAI ★ 2004

THE ORIGIN OF THE TAMIL VELALAS.[1]

Translated by V. J. TAMBIPILLAI.

[*Note by the Translator.*—This essay was composed in Tamil by the learned sub-editor of "Shen-Tamil" (the organ of the Tamil Sangam at Madura), Mr. M. Raghava Iyengar, and read by him on May 25, 1906, on the occasion of the great Annual Meeting of the Pundits of the Madura Tamil Sangam, the late lamented Mr. V. Kanakasabhai Pillai, B.A., B.L., of the Postal Department, Madras, being in the chair.

Every effort has been made to adhere strictly to the style and even the idiom of the original, except where a free rendering appeared to be necessary in order to bring out the exact meaning. I have added also, here and there, a few explanatory notes, which will, perhaps, be of some use and interest to the reader in following the arguments of the learned author.—*V. J. Tambipillai.*]

IT may sound strange, indeed, to the ears of some that whatever share of the glory of fostering Shen-Tamil[2] may have belonged to the Cheras,[3] the Pandiyas, and the Cholas,

---

[1] [The Editing Secretary is in no way responsible for the acceptance of this Paper.]

[2] Pure, unmixed Tamil.—V. J. T.

[3] The Cheras, the Choles, and the Pandiyas were the three most powerful of ancient Tamil kings. Their houses are supposed to have become extinct many centuries ago.—V. J. T.

there existed in former times, side by side with these, a community claiming, if not a greater, at least certainly an equal share of that glory. To those, however, who have an intimate acquaintance with old Tamil authors, this information will not be surprising. Upon inquiry conducted with regard to truth, it will become evident that the exceeding greatness of the position held by this community (in Tamil literature) was equalled only by that of the Tamil culture created by the triple kings [1] of the south. I refer above to a section of the ancient Tamil community known by the appellation of "Velir." [2] The larger number of "the last seven great Vallals" [3] of the Tamil country belonged to this race, and such was their munificence, it is said, that it obviated further begging on the part of those who had but once been the objects of it. It was to one of these seven great Vallals that the sacred poet [4] referred when he sang: "He will not give who has not the mind to give, even if one should call him Pari." Who was that prince of givers whose unrivalled reputation as a patron of the Tamil bards of his time drew upon him the jealous hatred [5] of the three kings? Except some general information, we have, as yet, very little knowledge in detail as to the origin and history of this important community.

---

[1] The Cheras, the Cholas, and the Pandiyas.—V. J. T.

[2] "Velir" is the plural form of "Vel." "Velalas" is only another form of it. The agricultural class among the Tamils are called by this name.—V. J. T.

[3] A person of lavish munificence is, in Tamil, called a "Vallal." The Tamil chiefs Ay, Pekan, Ori, Malayaman, Elini, Pari, and Nalli are known as "the last seven Vallals" of the Tamil land, and they lived about the time of the last Tamil Sangam held at Madura about twenty centuries ago.—V. J. T.

[4] Sundarar, a Sivite saint and poet, who lived in the 9th century A.D.—V. J. T.

[5] "Vel Pari was the ruler of a petty principality called 'Parambu. He was a bold and gay adventurer, simple-hearted and generous, and passionately fond of poetry. Every wandering minstrel was welcome in his mansion. The sons of song were nowhere petted and feasted as they were in Pari's palace. They found in him a union of all those virtues which they loved to praise in their rhapsodies: reckless courage, lavish liberality, and a gaiety which no reverse could check. He soon became their idol, and his fame spread throughout Tamilakam. The bards recounted, in glowing language, in the courts of the Chera,

Is it not a sacred duty of the sons of the Tamil land to take a small fraction of the interest, at least, in the Velir, which they evince in the study of the Cheras, the Pandiyas, and the Cholas as the great patrons of their national tongue in the past? It is, of course, to be admitted that the materials now available are scarcely so abundant as to secure a high degree of success in this investigation. Neither old books, nor writings of any other sort, chronicling the traditional history of the Vels, exist to-day, a few odes, or lines of poetry, composed and sung by some of the old Tamil bards in praise of their patrons, and which appear included in the anthologies[1] compiled by the last Tamil Sangam at Madura, being almost the sole accessible sources of light we have at present on this subject. Hardly possible as it is, then, to compile anything like a history of the Vels from these isolated and scanty materials, we shall, nevertheless, endeavour, with the help of such light as we possess, to explore, as best we can, the gloomy cell of their distant past, and lay before the public whatever discoveries we may chance to light upon.

In old poetical works in Tamil, then, a community called "Velir" is often mentioned side by side with the three great powers of the south, viz., the Cheras, the Pandiyas, and the Cholas. In "Purrananooru,"[2] "Pathittupaththu,"[3] &c.,

---

Chola, and Pandiya, the princely hospitality with which they were entertained by Pari. This excited the jealousy of the three kings, and they sent their forces to besiege Parambu. The defiles of the mountain passes with which Pari's followers were familiar were strictly guarded by them, and Pari, by his personal bravery, maintained, for some days, an unequal contest with the large and well-equipped army that surrounded him. At length, the enemies forced their way up the mountain and attacked Pari, who was killed in the encounter."—*Vide* "The Tamils Eighteen Hundred Years Ago," pp. 104, 105.—V. J. T.

[1] The works referred to are "Akam," "Purram," "Nattinai," "Kurantokai," "Pathittupaththu," &c., some of which have lately come out in print.—V. J. T.

[2] "Purrananooru," or "Purram," as it is sometimes called, is a collection of 400 odes composed by about 180 poets.—V. J. T.

[3] "Pathittupaththu" consists of ten poems by ten different poets. These works seem to be compilations from the works of the early Tamil poets which have long since become extinct.—V. J. T.

for instance, we find such passages as the following, viz.: "The renowned Venthar [1] and Velir," "the Venthar and Velir," "the Velir and the two great Venthar," &c. From these references, in which the "Velir" almost always appear in company with the three paramount rulers of Tamilakam,[2] it may fairly be concluded that, next to the kings themselves, the most honoured amongst the petty rulers and princes of the country were the chiefs of this "Velir" race. Moreover, the references to this people found in Tamil works as "the very ancient Velir" and the Velir who boasted of "an ancestry of forty-nine generations" must be held to imply that their settlement in South India dated from very ancient times.

Now, who were these "Vels," and what was their primitive habitat? Were they the kith and kin of the primitive Tamils, or foreign immigrants, of a later period? What is their place in the history and chronology of South India?

The learned Naccinarkiniyar,[3] in his commentary on the preface to "Tolkappiam,"[4] notices some of the traditions

---

[1] Kings.—V. J. T.

[2] The Tamil country. This is identical with the "Limirike" (Damirike) of the Greek writers Periplus and Ptolemy.—V. J. T.

[3] "The commentary of Naccinarkiniyar is the best and latest of all the existing commentaries on the grammar of Tolkappian. He was a learned Jain Brahman, and seems to have mastered Tamil and Sanscrit, and by writing commentaries on many great and important Tamil works has done a service to Tamil literature which Madhavacarya and Mallinathasuri have done for Sanscrit. In the colophons to the commentary, he is said to have been a native of Madura and born of the Bharadwaja gotra.

"There is a tradition which makes Naccinarkiniyar an elder contemporary of Parimelalagar, who, in his commentary on the 'Kural' of Tiruvalluvar, refers to a Bhoja king of Dhara who lived in the 11th century A.D."—*Vide* Report on a Search for Sanscrit and Tamil Manuscripts for the Years 1893-94, by M. Sheshagiri Sastri, M.A., Curator, Government Oriental Manuscripts Library, and Professor of Sanscrit and Comparative Philology, Presidency College, Madras, No. 2, pp. 107 and 110.

Recent researches have definitely fixed the 11th century A.D. as the upper limit of the period of this author.—V. J. T.

[4] "Tolkappiam" is the oldest Tamil grammar now extant. It was composed by a Brahman named Tolkappian, who lived, according to

current in the Tamil country in the remote past concerning the origin of the primitive "Vels" as follows, viz. :—

[1] "The gods assembling said among themselves, 'We being all gathered here in one place (on Mount Meru), Meru has gone down (by our combined weight), and the south has gone up, Agastiyar alone (amongst us all) is competent to reside in the south (in order to preserve the balance of the earth),' and so they entreated him; and he also consenting, went to Dwarapati, [2] and taking along with him the eighteen

---

Mr. Kanakasabhai Pillai, not earlier than the 3rd century of our era. The traditions, however, make him a contemporary of the Rishi Agastiyar of Vedic fame. The author above referred to has not given his reasons for assigning to him a later date.—*Vide* "Tamils Eighteen Hundred Years Ago," p. 116.—V. J. T.

[1] The following is a somewhat different reading of the same passage as quoted by the learned Shehagiri Sastri, M.A., viz. :—

"All the gods who had assembled on Mount Meru requested Agastiya to go to the south and remain there to keep up the balance when the whole earth had bent on the southern side owing to the weight of all the gods. Before he went to the south, Agastiya went to the Ganges and received the river Kaviri from her. He then proceeded to Jamadhadhagniyar (Sans. Jamadhagni) and got from him Tirunadhumagniyar (Sans. Tranadhumagni), who was Tolkappian himself. He married Lopamudraiyar, who was given to him by her brother Pulathiyanar (Sans. Pulastya). He went to Tuwarapati (Sans. Dwaraka) and took the eighteen kings of the line of Krisna, the Velirs of the eighteen families, and Aruvalars. He denuded the country of its forests, and made it inhabitable. He settled on Mount Pothiya, and having defeated Ravana by his skill in music, freed his habitation from the incursions of the Rakshasas."—Report on a Search for Sanscrit and Tamil Manuscripts for the Years 1893-94, No. 2, p. 109.—V. J. T.

[2] Same as Dwaraka. Its Tamil form is "Dwarai" or "Dwarakai." The reference to Ravana has, obviously, no connection with the context. Nachchar makes the same remarks in his comments on "Madura Kanchi." If the Ravana here referred to is identical with the Ravana slain by Rama, there is no reason for introducing him here after the time of lord Krishna.

The above observation obviously ignores the fact that the Puranic legends represent Ravana and Agastiyar, not only as contemporaries, but also as relatives, the latter being, according to one account, an uncle of the former. The "Ramayana" also makes Agastiyar a contemporary of Ravana, and makes express reference to the existence of the Pandiyan kingdom at the time the epic was composed.—V. J. T.

kings of the line of 'the supreme lord[1] who measured the earth with one foot,' together with eighteen crores of Vels and their dependents, and Aruvalar, migrated to the south, and depriving Ravana of his sovereignty over the Rakshasas by his superior skill in music, clearing the country of its forests, and making it fit for human habitation, finally took his abode on the hill of Pothíyil." [2]

What is apparently deserving of consideration in the above account is the information that the Muni Agastiyar[3] went to Dwarapati, and led from there a colony composed of kings and Vels of the race of Sri Krishna, to the south, and permanently settled them there. These traditions, though agreeing generally with the Puranic accounts of the migration of the Muni Agastiyar to South India, in their specific reference to his (*i.e.*, Agastiyar's) being accompanied by many kings and princes of the family of Sri Krishna, are entirely missed in the latter (*i.e.*, the Puranas). Be this as it may, it is noteworthy that our learned author once again refers, as follows, to the same story—as if to confirm his first statement—in his notes on another Sutram[4] of "Tolkappiam," namely :—

"The right to rule belongs also to the Vels of the eighteen

---

[1] This refers to Krishna as an incarnation of Vishnu. "According to Hindu mythology, Bali was an Asura emperor who, through his devotion and penance, defeated Indra, humbled the gods, and extended his authority over the three worlds. In order to restrain him, Vishnu, who was appealed to by the gods for protection, assumed his fifth incarnation, the form of a Brahman dwarf, the Vamana Avatara, and appearing before Bali, asked for only three paces of ground as a boon—which was granted. As the water conveying the gift fell into his hand, the dwarf's form expanded till it filled the world, and Vishnu, now manifesting himself, deprived Bali, in two strides, of heaven and earth, but on account of the virtues the latter possessed, left Patala, or the infernal regions, still in his dominion."—"Mysore Gazetteer," by R. Lewis Rice, C.I.E., M.R.A.S., p. 301. See under "Mahavalis."—V. J. T.

[2] A hill near the extreme south of the peninsula.

[3] "Muni" means "an ascetic."—V. J. T.

[4] *Vide* "Tolkappiam," chapter on "Poruladhikaram." The Maha Bharata frequently refers to "the eighteen clans or tribes of the Yadavas."—V. J. T.

"Aruvalar was the local name of the Naga tribes who inhabited Aruva and Aruva-Vadathalai (*i.e.*, North Aruva). The two provinces,

tribes or gotra whom the great Mathavan [1] (*i.e.*, the ascetic) of Malaya [2] brought along with the Narapatis [3] of the line of the Supreme Lord who measured the earth with one foot."

In the second passage the tribe of Aruvalar is omitted, while the Narapatis and the Vels are again mentioned as descended from the race of Sri Krishna, divided into eighteen tribes or clans, and entitled to the right of ruling. As Nachchar [4] makes this assertion, not once but twice, it seems a fair conclusion that there must have existed, in his day, sources of information on this matter which have, since then, disappeared. Unfortunately for us, however, he has not given us the authorities on which he relied in making these statements. Moreover, does not the statement sound astonishing that these

---

Aruva and North Aruva, were together known as Mavilankai or the Great Lanka. The capital of this province was Kachchi, the modern Kanchipuram. The whole of this country was inhabited by the Aruvalar, a nomadic tribe, who were also called Kurumbar. It was the Chola king, Karikal the Great, who first settled these wandering tribes."—" The Tamils Eighteen Hundred Years Ago," pp. 27, 44.

It is the opinion of Dr. Gustav Oppert that " Kuru " is the original form of the name " Kurumbar," which has also other forms, such as "Kurbar," "Kuruvar," &c., of which " Korama," " Kuruciyar," and " Kunbi" are but variants. The shepherd Kurumbas were very influential during the days of the Vijayanagara dynasty, the foundation of which is attributed to a Kuruba noble. The shepherd Kurumbas still call themselves " Yadavalu," *i.e.*, Yadavas. That the Kurumbars hold, like the Velir, the position of petty kings in the Tamil country is proved also by the following passage in "Divakaram," viz., " Velir, Purochar, Arattar, and Kurumbar are names of petty kings."

Again, the Kurubas of Mysore are known as "Cunabis" and " Ruddies,"—which fact connects them with the "Rattas" of Manyakheta, who were Yadavas. The dynasty of Vijayanagara is said to be an offshoot of the earlier royal family of Tuluva, *i.e.*, the Kadambas. Moreover, the words " Kurumpan " and " Kadampan " are, in Tamil, interchangeable, being vocables of the same meaning.

The above facts seem to show that the now much despised Kurubas are of high origin, being the modern representatives of the Aruvalar of the Tamil records.—V. J. T.

[1] An ascetic.—V. J. T.

[2] The Southern Ghats, but the peak of Pothiyil is here referred to.—V. J. T.

[3] "Narapatis" means " kings " or "rulers."—V. J. T.

[4] An abbreviated form of " Naccinarkiniyar."—V. J. T.

Vels of the Tamil country were of the same race to which Sri Krishna belonged? We propose, therefore, to use the information handed down by Nachchar as the first stepping-stone in our inquiry, and investigate whether this account of the Vels is so supported from any other quarter as to give it the status of genuine history.

If the Vels were, as stated by Nachchar, the kindred of Sri Krishna, who ruled over Dwaraka in olden times, we may safely say that they were Yadavas. For it is admitted on all hands that the tribe to which Sri Krishna belonged were all descendants [1] of "Yadu," and of the Lunar Vamsa, or race. If, then, the Vels were Yadavas who emigrated in

---

[1] "Yadu" was the eldest son of "Yayati" (by "Devyani"), one of the ancestors of the Pandavas. His family, increasing and multiplying, branched off into numerous separate clans, which gave birth to many distinguished kings. Thus, Sahasrajit, the eldest son of Yadu, was the founder of the Haihaya family, to which the great conqueror Kirta Viriya Arjuna belonged. The Thalajangas were also a section of this race. The most distinguished among the descendants of Kuroshtaka, the second son of Yadu, were Chashibindu, Chiyamaha, and Vidarba, from the last of whom the Vidarba family originated. The Chedi family originated from the third son of Vidarba. From Satuwika, a descendant of the second son of Vidarba, the Bhoja, Andhaka, and Vrishni families originated, and it was in the family of the Andhakas that Kannapiran (*i.e.*, lord Krishna) incarnated.

According to the Vishnu Parva of the "Harivamsa," Yadu was born of the Solar race. It says that Harjashya, king of Ayodhya, of the Solar race, married the daughter of Madhu, king of Madhuvana (*i.e.*, Mathura), and begat Yadu, from whom the Yadavas were descended.

It is stated in the "Ramayana" that Lavana, son of Madhu, a relative of Ravana, was ruling in Madhuvana at the time of Rama, and that Satrughna, younger brother of Rama, defeated him, and built the city of Mathura on the banks of the Yamuna. This story, considered together with the account given in the "Mahabharata" that Yadu was the progenitor of the Rakshasas, establishes a significant connection between the Yadavas of the classics and the despised aborigines of India, *i.e.*, the Yakshas and the Rakshasas.

The following is the genealogy of the Yadavas, as given in the Puranas :—

Chandra (Moon) begat Budha, Budha begat Ila, Ila begat Pururava, Pururava begat Ayu, Ayu begat Nahusha, Nahusha begat Yayati, Yayati begat Yadu, and Yadu was the progenitor of the Yadavas.

On reference to the genealogy of the Solar race, it will be found that Nahusha" appears in it as one of the ancient kings of that line also,

ancient times from Dwaraka, some notices of this fact must occur, in all probability, in old Tamil writings. But as no Tamil books of such ancient date as the times of Sri Krishna now exist, we are not likely to succeed in discovering any contemporary record of the event in the mass of Tamil literature now available. In the absence of any record of a contemporary date, it is a matter for which we ought to be very thankful that there are, at least, a few lines in some of the extant compositions of the poets of the last Sangam [1] at Madura which throw a good deal of light on the origin of the Vels. The following is an extract from an ode composed by a poet named "Kapilar" in praise of one of the Vel princes of his time named "Irung Ko [2] Vel," viz. :—

> "Thou, thou art the Vel of the Vels who, originating in the sacred thadavu of a Muni in the north, boast of a pedigree of forty-nine generations of Vels, since ruling over Dwaraka, glittering like gold, and surmounted by its copper fortress." [3]

According to the above passage the Vels were, originally, the ruling race of Dwaraka, who moved down to the south

---

and it may, therefore, be concluded that the Lunar race was, in reality, only an offshoot of the older Solar dynasty. This accounts, perhaps, for the fact that, while the Cholas claimed to be of the Solar line, the Pandiyas of Mathurai traced their descent from the Moon. It has also to be noted that there was a dynasty of Solar Pandiyas who held sway in various parts of South India in ancient times.—V. J. T.

[1] "The language and literature were under the Pandiyan kings the special charge of an academy of poets and savants analogous to the Académie Française, and the three epochs of the Academy called the First, Second, and Third Sangams are the great landmarks in ancient Tamil history. The literature of the first two epochs has perished save one work, a grammatical work called 'Tolkappiam,' and which is to Tamil what 'Paniniyam' (Ashtadhyayi) is to Sanscrit. The loss of the literature is attributed to the destruction by the sea at successive periods of the two earliest Pandiyan capitals, old Madura and Kapadapuram. Of the works of the third period which have survived the best known is the 'Kural' of Tiruvalluvar, a poem of singular literary and ethical value which has been translated into most of the European languages."—*Vide* "Report on Ceylon Census, 1901." vol. I., p. 80, para. 28.—V. J. T.

[2] "Ko" means "a king."— V. J. T.

[3] *Vide* "Purrananooru," ode No. 201.—V. J. T.

in later times, and founded kingdoms for themselves in the Dravida[1] country. We have now to admit that the statement of Nachchar concerning the origin of the Vels receives full confirmation, in one important point, from a classical authority of the first rank.

Although the fact that the Vels were settlers from Dwaraka is supported, as shown above, by a classical authority of great weight, it will be difficult to cite any passage from the Tamil classics to prove that they belonged also to the Yadava race.[2] But we may call in the help of the Puranas here. These state that the descendants of "Yadu" first settled in the regions watered by the Ganges; that, in course of time,

---

[1] "Dravida" is the name by which the Tamil country and people are known in Sanscrit literature. "Dravidam" means also the Tamil language, and is, evidently, a corruption of "Tamilam," its present form being "Tamil."—V. J. T.

[2] If "Yadava" be the ancient name of the Tamil Velalas, it appears to me to be most strange that it does not occur either in the Tamil books or in the traditional recollections of the agricultural Tamilas. May not the difficulty be explained away by supposing it to be a Sanscrit equivalent of a Tamil name ?

The Yadavas appear in the "Maha Bharata" under more than one appellation. They were called "Suras," "Somakas," "Madhus," "Vrishnis," &c., and these names, apparently, convey the same meaning. It will be admitted that the words "Yadu," "Madhu," and "Sura" are synonyms, and mean "toddy" or "palm-wine." Can it be that the Yadavas were a toddy-drawing race, and hence their names, such as the "Suras," "Madhus," &c.? The Puranic story, that they were so called on account of their being descended from a progenitor known by the name of "Yadu," is easily explained as an invention of later philology.

In modern Dravida there are several tribes whose principal occupation is that of cultivating palm trees and extracting toddy from them. Now it is remarkable that a Vel prince by the name of Vel Avik Ko Perum Pekan, or The Great Vel King Pekan of the race of Aviyar, is mentioned in old Tamil literature as a great patron of Tamil poets. Paiki or Paika is the name of the highest section of the Todas of the Nilgiris, as well as of a section of the people occupying the Nagar Malnad of Canara. Another tribe occupying the district on the north of Hanovar, also in Canara, is known as Kumara Paika. The "Paikas" are also found in Vizagapatam and Orissa, those of the former country being known also as "Sandi." These races of "Paikas" are all, it has to be noted, toddy-drawers by profession, although they are agriculturists to a greater or less extent.

their race having become very numerous, Sri Krishna,[1] in order to further its prosperity, led a large colony of it to the shore of the western ocean, founded Dwaraka, and clearing the jungles and forests of the surrounding districts, and preparing the ground for cultivation and human residence, settled his Yadava followers on them, and himself ruled over the new kingdom. From the "Maha Bharata" we also learn that, shortly before the death of Sri Krishna a civil war broke out,[2] and raged among the Yadavas of Dwaraka, in which large numbers of them perished, while, of the rest, the majority left for other places; and that the districts to the south of the Godaveri were largely inhabited by the Yadavas. From these accounts it is obvious that the Yadavas were a race fond of colonizing, that they originally inhabited[3] the Gangetic regions, and that thence they removed to that part of India now known as Maharashtra. If the above have any foundation in fact, it is nothing incredible that the Yadavas, who so settled in Maharashtra, should have, as time went on,

---

The Tamil records mention also another Vel prince who belonged to the Aviyar race, who was the lord of Pothiyil, the traditional seat of the sage Agastiyar, I mean the prince "Ay Andiran," one of the last seven Vallals of the Tamil country.

From the above it is clear that there were sections of people whose occupation was mainly that of preparing intoxicating beverages for the use of the liquor-loving Yadavas, and who, nevertheless, belonged to the very race to which the Tamil Vels belonged. In fact, the words Ilar, Cherar, Konkar, Yadavar, and Surar are only different designations of the same class of people, and are so strictly synonymous that they can be used interchangeably with the utmost freedom.—V. J. T.

[1] Krishna and his clansmen were, at first, settled in the kingdom of Mathura. But, subsequently, through fear of the Magadha king, Jarasandha, father-in-law of Kansa whom Krishna had slain, they fled towards the west, and founded Dwaraka.—*Vide* "Maha Bharata," "Sabha Parva," chap. XIV., slokas 48–55.—V. J. T.

[2] An account of this civil war is given in the "Mushala Parva" of the "Maha Bharata." The origin of the war is attributed to drunkenness, to which they had become so fatally addicted that Krishna was obliged to pass a law enforcing capital sentence on all those found drunk.—V. J. T.

[3] The Velalas were called Gangakula or Ganga Vamsa, because they derived their descent from the powerful tribe of Gangaridæ which inhabited the valley of the Ganges, as mentioned by Pliny and Ptolemy. —*Vide* "The Tamils Eighteen Hundred Years Ago," p. 114.—V. J. T.

moved down further south, and taken possession of the forest tracts of the Tamil country. Although no direct reference is to be found in the Sanscrit works to the emigration of the Yadavas to South India, it seems but fair to take the above meagre, but clear, hints as, at least, an indirect allusion to that event. I would here draw attention to what a modern writer of world-wide reputation has written on this matter. The learned Romesh Chunder Dutt, in his "Civilization of Ancient India," writes [1] to the following effect, viz.: "The Yadavas who acknowledged the leadership of Krishna quitted Mathura,[2] and founded a colony in Dwaraka in Gurjara; [3] they did not, however, stay there for a long time; fighting among themselves, most of them quitted Dwaraka, and voyaged to other places by sea, and those who thus left Dwaraka are believed to have reached South India, and founded a new kingdom there." It is easy to see how closely this tallies with what Nachchar has recorded concerning the primitive Vels. If it be said, however, that Mr. Dutt's statement may have been based, possibly, on what some South Indian author or writer had previously published, it must suffice to answer that no South Indian writer has as yet advanced the opinion that the Vels were Yadavas by race. The conclusion seems inevitable, therefore, that the learned historian has relied upon some oral or written traditions current in North India, corresponding to that current in the south. Our commentator's account of the ancestors of the Tamil Vels being thus corroborated by an independent writer of admitted scholarship, it may fairly be conceded that it is, at least, not open to any serious objection.

But there is another proof that the Vels were settlers from the north, and members of the Yadava race. Many of us are, perhaps, aware that a line of rulers known as "Hoysalas" [4] to their contemporaries, invading Mysore about nine hundred

---

[1] Dutt's "Ancient India," p. 219.

[2] Now called "Muttra" in Northern India.

[3] Guzerat.

[4] For an account of this dynasty, please see "Gazetteer of Mysore," by Lewis Rice, "Historical Period." The Hoysalas belonged to the Ganga Vamsa.—V. J. T.

years ago, conquered, and ruled over it, from their capital which they named "Dwarasamudra."[1] They were natives of Gurjara, and Yadavas by race. They were also known as "Belalas" to the Canarese. That these "Belala" kings were invaders from Gurjara, and of the Yadava Vamsa, are facts of history. The resemblance between "Belala" and the Tamil name "Velala" is a significant fact that we should keep in mind in this inquiry. Moreover, a city founded by these Belala Yadavas is still known by the name of "Velur" or "Velapuram."[2] We may gather from these facts that, although the Hoysala Yadavas were, in Canarese, called "Belalas," the correct form of their name is that found in common usage among the Tamils, viz., "Velala," and that the name "Vel" found in the old Tamil classics was, also, used to designate them. The learned Mr. V. Kanakasabhai Pillai, B.A., B.L., in his most valuable work entitled "The History of the Tamils Eighteen Hundred Years Ago,"[3] though not calling the Tamil Velalas and the Belalas of Dwarasamudra, Yadavas, has, nevertheless, treated them as belonging to the same race.[4]

There is yet another fact that leads us to believe that the Belalas of Dwarasamudra and the ancient Vels of the Tamil country were members of one and the same race. I have elsewhere referred to an old Tamil bard who speaks of "Irung Ko Vel" as a descendant of the Vels who originally ruled in Gurjara. This bard, in both his odes in praise of the Vel chief, calls him by the name "Pulikadimal,"[5] which the commentator of "Purrananooru" passes over without saying

---

[1] This is situated in Mysore.

[2] This is now known as "Halabidu."

[3] *Vide* "Tamils Eighteen Hundred Years Ago," p. 114. The Bellal dynasty which ruled over "Gangavadi" is identical with the Hoysalas.—V. J. T.

[4] "In the Canarese country the Velalas founded the Bellal dynasty, which ruled that country for several centuries. A portion of Mysore which was peopled mostly by the Velalas was called Gangavadi in the tenth and eleventh centuries of the Christian era. Another dynasty of the kings of this tribe which ruled Orissa in the eleventh and twelfth centuries was known as the Gangavamsas."—V. J. T.

[5] The Mal or lord who killed the tiger.—V. J. T.

anything more as to its meaning, or origin, than barely stating it to be one of that chief's names. Even the Sangam literature now accessible does not afford us any clue to the discovery of the reason of this name as applied to the Vel prince by the poet Kapilar. In these circumstances, it must be a matter of extreme interest to us that a story, related about the old Belala princes of Mysore, furnishes us with a very satisfactory explanation of its origination, and establishes beyond doubt the racial identity of these two great peoples. It has been already mentioned that the Belalas of Dwarasamudra were called also the "Hoysalas." In the history of the kings of Kongu, as well as in English books of recent dates, the origin of the word "Hoysala" is thus explained, viz.: "While Tabangar, an ascetic, was performing his penances in a forest, a tiger, appearing suddenly, was about to spring upon him, when the terrified ascetic seeing 'Sala,' a prince of the Yadava race, who had just arrived there on a hunting excursion, called upon him to slay it, and he, obeying the Muni's order, instantly shot it down with an arrow. On this account it was that his (*i.e.*, Sala's) descendants were called 'Hoysalas'[1] in the Canarese language."[2] This story does certainly contain, it appears to me, the true solution of the origin of the name "Pulikadimal,"[3] applied by the Tamil bard to Irung Ko Vel, whose ancestors also, like the Belalas of Dwarasamudra, were originally natives of Gurjara. Is it not because these princes were descended from a common ancestor who risked his own life by fighting a tiger single handed

---

[1] "Hoysala" is said to mean "kill, Sala," in Canarese.—V. J. T.

[2] Mr. Lewis Rice gives a somewhat different version of the same legend. "Going one day to worship Vasantika, his family goddess, whose temple was in the forest near Sasakapura, his devotions were interrupted by a tiger which bounded out of the jungle glaring with rage. The yati or priest of the temple snatching up a salaki (a slender iron rod) gave it to the chief, saying in the Karnatika language, 'Hoy, Sala' (strike Sala), on which the latter discharged the weapon with such force at the tiger as to kill him on the spot. From this circumstance he adopted the name Hoysala, formed from the words of the yati's exclamation, and the dynasty so called and descended from him had a tiger as the device on the flag."—*Vide* p. 335, "Mysore Gazetteer," see under "History." —V. J. T.

[3] *Vide* "Purrananooru," ode No. 202.—V. J. T.

in order to save the life of a weak and helpless ascetic who had appealed to him for protection that they were called "Hoysala" and "Pulikadimal"—names implying, or explained, as it can be distinctly seen, by that story? These facts put together obviously constitute an irresistible array of evidence that the Tamil Velir of two thousand years ago, and the people called by the Canarese "Belalas" of nine hundred years ago, were identical by race, rank, and name, and belonged to the Yadava race of ancient India.

We shall now inquire into the history of the names "Vel" and "Velala," by which the Yadavas of ancient Tamilakam, and the Yadavas of Dwarasamudra, were respectively called. Among the old dynasties which held sway over the countries lying to the south of the Vindhyas there was one known as "the Chalukkyas,"[1] whose primitive country was Gurjara and the districts immediately to the south of it. At first they established their sovereignty in the western portion of the Deccan. But later, a branch of them took possession of the countries on the eastern coast, and also ruled over some portions of the south. In order to distinguish the one from the other, the senior branch of the Chalukkyas was called "the Western Chalukkyas," and the junior branch "the Eastern Chalukkyas." Of these, the Chalukkyas who ruled over a portion of the Tamil country would appear to have been known to the old Tamil authors as "Velpula Arasar," *i.e.*, the kings of Velpulam,[2] or the Vel country. In the Tamil lexicon "Divakaram," for instance, we find the following passage, namely: "Velpula Arasar Chalukku Vendar," which means "Velpula kings are identical with the Chalukku monarchs." As "Divakaram" was compiled under the patronage of "Ambarkilan Chendanar," whose praises are said, in the lexicon itself, to have been sung by the poetess "Auvvaiyar" of the

---

[1] For a brief history of the Chalukkya dynasty please refer to "Gazetteer of Mysore," by Mr. Lewis Rice.

[2] From this it will be seen that the country of Maharashtra was known to the ancient Tamils as "Velpulam." The tract about Balabhipura (in Kathiawar) and northward is termed "Bhal," probably from the tribe of "Balla."—*Vide* Tod's "Annals of Rajasthan," vol. I., p. 219. If "Venadu," *i.e.*, "Vel Nadu" of old Tamil literature, was identical with the "Velpulam" or "Vel country of the

last Sangam, it is clear that its compilation dates as far back as 1,800 years ago. Although no inscription of the Chalukkyas of a date anterior to the fifth century A.D. has as yet been discovered, the fact of their being mentioned in "Divakaram"[1] of the second century A.D. is to be considered a strong proof of their earlier existence as a ruling race. By "Velpulam" we ought to understand "Gurjara" and the adjacent districts, which correspond more or less exactly to the modern "Maharashtra," and it was, no doubt, because the

---

Chalukkya rulers, it seems an easy conclusion that there were extensive settlements of the Dravidian races in the peninsula of Guzerat and in Saurashtra in very ancient times. The learned author of the "Gazetteer of Mysore" has made the following interesting remarks, namely:—

"They (the Dravidians) may be identified with the Zend Turanians ('an' signifying God in that language) and with the maritime traders called 'Toursha' and 'Tursene' or 'Tyrrhenians' mentioned in Egyptian and Greek records. Their first great trading port was Dwaraka in the peninsula of Kathiawar, other exporting harbours being Surparaka at the mouth of the Tapti and Barygaza at the mouth of the Narmada. They made settlements at the holy island of Dilmun in the Persian Gulf and at Eridu near the mouth of the Euphrates." —*Vide* "Gazetteer of Mysore," p. 209.—V. J. T.

[1] "Divakaram," the oldest Tamil lexicon now extant, was written by a Tamil noble called Sendan, chief of a place called Ambal. The popular opinion that it was written by one Divakaramuni, father of Pingalar who composed the Tamil lexicon bearing his name, viz., "Pingalandai," seems to rest on no solid foundation. The work is divided into twelve chapters, at the end of each of which there is a stanza praising the accomplishments and literary eminence of the author, Sendan, and in one of these stanzas it is expressly stated that the lexicon was composed by this learned noble. Not one of the twelve stanzas refer to Divakaramuni as the author of the work, which is very strange, and requires explanation if we are to suppose that he was the real author who compiled the lexicon. These stanzas are obviously later additions, and if we may assume that they were incorporated with the work by Divakaran, who possibly revised and edited it, the origin of the tradition associating his name with it is satisfactorily explained.

Pingalar was a son of one Divakarar, and wrote a lexicon which is extant, known as "Pingalam" or "Pingalandai." The late Mr. Sheshagiri Sastri, M.A., writes as follows as to the date of its composition, viz.:—

"He (Pingalar) mentions the word 'Pallava' among the synonyms of 'the mean,' from which we have to understand that, after the downfall of the Pallava kingdom at Kanchi, the Pallavas were so

Chalukkya rulers had come from this country, they were known as "Velpula Arasar," *i.e.*, kings of Velpulam, to the ancient Tamils.

It is now obvious why the Yadavas who settled in Tamilakam in very ancient times, and the Hoysala Yadavas of Dwarasamudra who arrived comparatively in recent times, were known as Vels and Velalas, respectively, to the older inhabitants of Dravida. The reason is that they were inhabitants of Velpulam [1] prior to their settlement in the south.

Not only are the kings of the Chalukkyas defined, as elsewhere mentioned, as "Velpula Arasar," in the Tamil lexicons, but the name Vel also is expressly stated to have belonged to them, as will appear from the following passage in "Pinkalandai":—

"Vel means either the slayer of Taraka,[2] the king of the Chalukkyas, or the god of love."

It seems a legitimate conclusion, therefore, that it is because the Chalukkyas entered the Tamil country from Velpulam that they were called Vels. But we possess evidence to prove that they too were, like the Velir of Tamilakam, an offshoot of the illustrious race of Yadavas. It is a historical

---

persecuted by their enemies that the very name 'Pallava' became a synonym for 'the mean.' He also refers to the Chalukkya kings. From these references we can infer that the lexicon was written after the overthrow of the 'Pallavas,' and after the establishment of the Western Chalukkya kingdom about the 8th century A.D."—*Vide* his Report on Manuscripts, No. 2, p. 119.

The lower limit for the period of Pingalandai may, I think, be fixed with tolerable certainty. The Tamil grammar "Nannul," written by Pavanandimunivar under the patronage of a king named "Siyagangan," refers to Pingalam. If this "Siyagangan" may be supposed to be the same as the "Siyagangan" of the South Indian inscriptions, who was a contemporary of the Chola king Kulotunga III. (1178 A.D. to 1211 A.D.), the third quarter of the 12th century is the latest possible date that can be assigned to the lexicon in question.—*Vide* Epigraphical Reports, Government of Madras, Nos. 833, 834, Public, dated August 22, 1900.—V. J. T.

[1] It is most interesting to note here that the "Mahavansa," the Sinhalese chronicle, states that Vijaya, the first Sinhalese king, and his comrades, were natives of Lada, or Southern Gujerat, and that they intermarried with the Tamils of the Pandiyan country.—V. J. T.

[2] Kartikeya, or Skanda.—V. J. T.

fact that the Chalukkyas [1] inhabited primitively, as did the Yadavas of Tamilakam, the regions of the Ganges in the north, and their emblem, [2] agreeably with this fact, was the Gunga and the Yamuna, and they belonged to the Lunar race. Moreover, the appellation "Vallabha," [3] frequently used for the Yadavas in "Vishnupuranam," appears appended to the names of the Chalukkya rulers in their inscriptions, as in the names, for instance, "Pulikesi Vallabha" and "Kirti Varma Vallabha." This is a clear proof that the Chalukkyas were Yadavas by race. Further, the students of Indian archæology also say that the Chalukkyas were a branch of the Andhra emperors of ancient Maghada, who, it is held, were a mighty race even before the time of king Asoka, and that the Kalachuris,[4] the descendants of Vikramarka, the Kakatiyas [5] of Orissa, and the Yadava Narapatis of Vijayanagaram, were only offshoots of the same great Andhra race. If the Narapatis of Vijayanagaram, who called themselves Yadavas, were, as above stated, a branch of the ancient Andhra race, it follows then, as a logical sequence, that the Chalukkyas, who were also a branch of the Andhra race, were likewise Yadavas by descent. A proof still more convincing of the racial identity of the Vels of Tamilakam and the Chalukkyas, is

---

[1] For a brief history of the Chalukkyas, please see "Gazetteer of Mysore," by Mr. Rice.—V. J. T.

[2] The Gunga and the Yamuna were the emblems of the Guptas. The Chalukkyas defeated the Guptas in a pitched battle, and in memory of the great victory added the emblem of the conquered foe to their own, which was the figure of a boar.—V. J. T.

[3] "Vallabha" means those who roam about, "Vala-samvaranam," to come round. This appellation was given to the Yadavas on account of their roving habits after their herds of cattle in the various districts they had occupied.

[4] The Kalachuris were of Haiheya descent. According to the Puranas the Haiheyas were a section of the Yadavas. "Professor H. H. Wilson imagines them to be," says Mr. Lewis Rice, "a foreign tribe, and inclines with Tod to the opinion that they may have been of Scythian origin, and perhaps connected with a race of similar name who first gave monarchs to China."—See the "Gazetteer of Mysore," p. 274, "History, Legendary Period." The names Nissankamalla and Apratimalla occur among the names of these kings.—V. J. T.

[5] These kings ruled Orissa about 800 years ago, and were connected with the earlier Gunga dynasty of Mysore.—V. J. T.

furnished by the following account of the origin of the latter, which is given on page 339 of the second part of the first volume of the "Gazetteer of Bombay":—

> "In the north, an ascetic, named Harita Panchachika, was engaged in performing a sacrifice; and as he poured his oblations into the sacrificial hole, a king issued forth from his holy or sacred pot which, in Sanscrit, is called 'Chulukam,' and as he appeared in a 'Chulukam' he was called "Chulukan" by his contemporaries. But, in later times, his descendants, who were at first known as 'Chulukas,' came to be called 'Chalukkas,' 'Châlukkyas,' and 'Chálukkyas,' these names being only corruptions of the primitive form of their name." [1]

It is a matter over which we should heartily rejoice indeed that the above legend of the origin of the Chalukkyas is strictly identical with the story of the origin of the Vels of the Tamil

---

[1] Chalikyas, Chalkyas, Chalukkyas, and Chaulukyas. Tradition—as recorded in a stone tablet inscription at the temple of Lokesvaradeva, at Handarike, in the Haidarabad territories—states that the Chalukkyas sprang from a spray of a water-pot (Chulka, Chuluka, Chaluka) when Hariti, who wore five tufts of hair on his head, was pouring out a libation to the gods.—"Ind. Ant.," vol. VI., p. 74.

According to Bilhana, in his "Vikramankakavya," Brahma was once engaged in his *sandhya* devotions, when Indra came to him to complain of the growing godlessness on earth, and begged him to put an end to it by creating a hero who would be a terror to the evil-doers. On hearing this request, the creator directed his looks towards his *chuluka*, or water-vessel, and from it sprang a handsome warrior fit to protect the three worlds. From him descended the Chalukkyas. Harita was the first progenitor, and then Manavya arose.—"Ind. Ant.," vol. V., p. 317.

"I do not doubt," says Dr. G. Buhler, "that Chaulikyas (this form occurs in the inscriptions of the Gujarati branch of the Chalukyas) and Chalukyas are only dialectic variations of the same name."—"Ind. Ant.," vol. VI., p. 182.

It must be admitted, I incline to think, that the legend of the progenitor of the Chalukkyas issuing out of the sacred jar or pot of a Muni was originally suggested by the name of the tribe, of which those above noticed are modified forms, more or less, of a later date. The form "Chuluka" is, of course, very easily extracted, philologically, from "Chaulukya," but it does not occur in any of the Chalukya grants hitherto discovered. As it must be conceded, however, that the form of the name must have been such as to suggest the

country. This can be seen from the following extract of the ode sung by the bard Kapilar to which attention has already been drawn, namely :—

"Thou, thou art the Vel of the Vels who, appearing in the sacred Thadavu[1] of an ascetic in the north, count forty-nine generations of Vels, since ruling over Dwaraka, glittering like gold, and surmounted by its copper fortress."

---

idea of a "jar-born" race for the Chalukkyas, it seems reasonable to infer that a word signifying "a jar" or "a pot" must have been present in the ancient form of the name. We have in Tamil the words "Chal," "Chalikai," and "Chadi," all of which mean "a jar" or "a pot," but it may be objected that the Chalukkyas being an Aryan race, any explanation based on the Tamil language cannot be held to meet the case. However this may be, the Tamil words above noticed cannot but strike any impartial judge as affording a key to the solution of the origin of the legend in question. There is also another account of the origin of the name Chalukkya, which is that "Chalooka," the progenitor of the Chalukkyas, was formed in the palm (chaloo, Tamil சாலு) of the presiding priest at the Fire Fountain, and his descendants were, on that account, designated "Chalukyas." "Caluka" or "Culaka" signifies, says also Dr. Oppert, "a hollowed hand to receive water."—*Vide* Tod's "Rajasthan," vol. II., p. 440.—V. J. T.

The Chalukkyas were known also as "Chaluvar" to the Tamils, from "Chaluvam" (*i.e.*, Salva, the northern part of Guzerat), the name of the country from which they came down to the south, *vide* Dr. Rottler's Tamil-English Dictionary. The sage Agastiyar who is said to have accompanied the Pandiyan to Dravida was, no doubt, a distinguished scion of this race, as the story of his "springing from a pot" unmistakably indicates.—V. J. T.

[1] The commentator of "Purrananooru" interprets the word "Thadavu" not as meaning a pot, but a sacrificial hole, and so connects the Vels with the modern "fire races" of the north, namely, Cauhan, Caluk or Calukya (Solanki), Pramara, and Parihara. The caste of the Fire Races (called also Vanniyas or Agnikulas) in South India includes the Anuppar, Bailagar, Dèvadigar, Kallar, Maravar, Masadigar, Bantar, Mupar, Nattampadis, Padaiachchis, Parivarams, Uppiliyar, Udaiyar, and Vanniyar. According to Lieutenant-Colonel Tod, the Agnikulas of Hindostan are identical with the Scythic race which invaded India two centuries before Christ.—*Vide* his "Annals of Rajasthan," vol. I., p. 90. The Scythic race here referred to is, evidently, the "Sakas," called also the Yuei-chi by the Chinese, who were the masters of Northern India in the first century A.D.

Drs. Gustav Oppert and Fr. Buchanan agree with Colonel Tod that the Agnikulas of India are of non-Aryan origin.—*Vide* "The Original Inhabitants of Bharatavarsha," chap. VI., on the Agnikulas.—V. J. T.

Inasmuch as the designation of Vel, and the story of miraculous birth in the sacred pot of a Muni in the north, is thus seen to have been of common application to the Velir and the Chalukkyas, it is concluded that they were born of the same race, and offshoots of the Yadava class of it. The Puranas and the epics do not contain,[1] it is to be admitted, any passage referring to the birth of the first Yadava in the sacred pot of an ascetic (but this does not matter, as it does not affect our investigation). In addition to what has been said above, there is one more excellent proof of the racial identity of Vels and Chalukkyas. We learn from the Greek traveller Pliny that the Andhras were an imperial race about the commencement of the Christian era. Now, that it was to the Chalukkyas, who were a section of the Andhras, that the early Tamils gave the name Velir is proved by the name "Andiran" (அண்டிரன்), which is found applied to the great Vallal "Vel Ay" in the Tamil records. Assuming that "Vel Ay" was an "Andhra" by race, his designation "Andiran" (அண்டிரன்) can be easily explained as a modified form of "Andhran," especially as the word "Andiran" is perfectly meaningless in Tamil. To the ancient Greeks, the kings of the Andhras would appear to have been known as "Andorea"[2] (அண்டிரேயர்).

---

[1] The names "Kudamuni"—the pot-born ascetic—and "Kumbasambahva"—he who was born of a pot—assigned to the Rishi Agastiyar in the Puranic traditions, may well be taken to be a direct reference to this legend.—V. J. T.

[2] In old Sanscrit literature the Andhras are spoken of as an impure tribe. In the "Aitareya Brahmana," for instance, the Pulindas, the Andhras, Pundras, Sabaras, and Mutibas are said to be the offspring of the cursed elder sons of Visvamitra, while, in "Amarakosha," the oldest Sanscrit lexicon now extant, the "Bheda, Kirata, Sabara, and Pulinda" races appear included among the "Mleccha Jatis." The mere fact of the Andhras being mentioned as a race of common origin with such admittedly aboriginal tribes as the Sabaras and the Pulindas affords strong ground for regarding them as a non-Aryan people. The Andhras were a race closely akin, I am inclined to think, to the modern inhabitants of Telingana, *i.e.*, the Telugu country, which, as well as the language spoken there, is even now known as "Andhram."

The kings of the Andhras call themselves "Haritiputras," *i.e.*, "the sons of Hariti," in their inscriptions. "Hariti" is one of the progenitors of the Chalukkyas.

The facts above set forth demonstrate that the statement advanced by the erudite Nachchar, namely, that the community of Velir were the kindred of Sri Krishna, who quitted Dwaraka and settled in the south, is one that receives full and ample support from many well-known and authoritative sources.

Again, the Tamil classics state that the "Shen-Tamil" Nadu, *i.e.*, the country in which pure Tamil was spoken and cultivated, was surrounded by twelve Nadus, or countries, in which "Kodun-Tamil," *i.e.*, corrupt Tamil, was spoken, and that, of these, "Venadu" was one. I incline to think that this Venadu was no other than Velpulam,[1] the old home of the Yadavas, which has already been pointed out to be that part of the country lying to the north of what is now called Konkanam. That this country, viz., Konkanam, was inhabited by a Tamil-speaking population in ancient times is established by the odes sung by old Tamil bards in praise of Vel Konkanam Kilan, some of which have luckily found place in the Sangam anthology of "Purrananooru."[2] As Venadu lay next to Konkanam, which was a Tamil country, bands of Tamils moved about and settled there, as may well be expected in course of time, and the Tamils who thus settled spoke a vulgar patois of their mother tongue—which was hence called "Kodun-Tamil" by the pure Tamil-speaking people of the extreme south. It has, therefore, to be supposed that, although Venadu, which belonged to the Yadavas,[3] was

---

The Andhras are called "Andræ Indi" in the Pentigerian Tables, and "Gens Andaræ" by Pliny.—V. J. T.

[1] The Sanscrit pundits of old thought that there was no essential difference between the leading languages spoken in the countries lying to the south of the Vindhyas. So they called the Tamil, the Andhra, Karnataka, Maratha, and the Gurjara languages as "the five Dravidas." It is, therefore, not improbable that Tamil was the original language not only of Konkanam but also of Gurjara. According to an address delivered by Mr. Kanagasabhai Pillai, B.A., B.L., before the Tamil Sangam at Madura in 1906, there were numerous Tamil settlements round about Rajagriha, the capital of Magadha, about the 7th century B.C.—V. J. T.

[2] *Vide* "Purrananooru," odes Nos. 154, 155, and 156.

[3] It seems indeed very difficult to believe that the Pandiyas were, at any time, a people speaking any language other than Tamil. The

not wholly a Tamil-speaking country, the inhabitants of Shen-Tamil Nadu reckoned it to be a Kodun-Tamil Nadu on account of the prevalence of Tamil in some portions of it. "Venadu" means then, as above explained, "the Vel Nadu," or the Vel country, and not the "Ven" country, as later, or modern usage, would have it. How this error has occurred may be easily explained as follows; namely, Venadu is a compound Tamil vocable that may be resolved either into Ven and Nadu, or into Vel and Nadu. As later Tamil pundits adopted the former method of resolving the compound word, the use of Ven, in place of Vel, consequently got into Tamil literature.[1]

I now propose to investigate the date when the first ancestors of the Vels migrated from Velpulam and settled in Dravida. If it be true that it was, as indicated in the tradition mentioned by Nachchar, posterior to the age of Sri Krishna,

---

district of Mathurai which formed the core and centre of the Shen-Tamil, *i.e.*, the pure-Tamil speaking Nadu or country, was always known as the first and most ancient seat of the Pandiyas in Southern India, and nothing but a reversal of the natural order of things could convert a colony of Sanscrit-speaking men and women into a population so jealous of the purity of a Mlechcha tongue, hated and despised as it must have been by the other members of their race, that that portion of the peninsula occupied by them came to be known, from very early times, as "the Tamil country" *par excellence*, and the kings who ruled over them as "the Tamil kings," whose pride it was to cherish the purest dialect of the ancient language of Southern India. But an examination of the facts of the case would clearly indicate that this is not the right solution of the problem. I have already referred to the fact that Agastiyar himself was a "Vel" by caste. He was also a relative, according to the Sanscrit Puranas, of Ravana, the Yaksha or Rakshasa king of Lanka. Moreover, the Sanscrit records state that "Yadu" was the progenitor of the Yadavas as well as of the Rakshasas. The Shanars of Tinnevely claim, till to-day, an ancient connection with the Rakshasas of Lanka, and as the Dravidian affinities of these people have never yet been questioned, it may fairly be concluded that the ancient inhabitants of Gurjara were Tamil people, whose kings claimed descent from the sun and moon.—V. J. T.

[1] According to the author of "The Tamils Eighteen Hundred Years Ago" Venadu meant "the bamboo land," from "Ven," *i.e.*, bamboo, with which it abounded, and lay to the south-west of Pandi-Nadu, between Periyar and Cape Comorin, and bordering on the Arabian Sea. —See chap. II., on "The geography of Tamilakam."

one may then safely state it to be later than the time of the Bharata war. We are also in possession of a few data that enable us to fix more definitely the chronological limits of this event. As already mentioned, the bard Kapilar, in the ode of his addressed to the Vel chief Irung Ko Vel, refers to him as the forty-ninth in descent from his ancestor who last ruled at Dwaraka. This is, evidently, what was generally known concerning the ancestry and origin of the Vel chief in the learned circles of the time of this poet. Now, by allowing a reasonable average length of time for each of the forty-nine ancestors of the Vel, it will not be difficult to calculate the approximate date on which his first ancestor set foot on the soil of the Tamil country. According to Vishnu and Matsya Puranas, thirty-three kings of the line of Pali-Puchchaka ruled over Aryavarta for 486 years, and ten kings of the Maurya line for 137 years. This yields an average of fifteen years for the kings of the former line and fourteen years for those of the second. Turning our attention to the ruling dynasties of other countries, say to the royal family, for instance, of Japan, which is, at this moment, the cynosure of the whole civilized world, we find that her present absolute ruler, Mutsuhito, is the 123rd in regular descent and succession from Jimmu Tenno, the first absolute monarch of the line, who flourished, according to the historical records of Japan, about 2,500 years ago. Now, by dividing 2,500 years amongst 123 rulers, an average of 25 years is obtained for each of the past kings of Japan. In the case, likewise, of the ruling houses of Europe, the cold climate of which is conducive to longevity, the average length of reign is found to be 23 years for the British kings, 24 years for the French, 23 years for the German, and 19 years for the Russian sovereigns.[1] Of these averages, taking that obtained for the rulers of Japan, where the conditions of life are almost the same as in India, as a suitable basis of calculation in the case of the forty-nine Vel rulers above referred to, the date of emigration of the first Vel chief to Dravida is ascertained to be about 1,029 years anterior to the time of

---

[1] "The Chronology of Ancient India," by Velandai Gopala Iyer, B.A., p. 65.

Irung Ko Vel, who was sung by the bard Kapilar of the last Sangam. As Irung Ko Vel flourished about 1,800 years ago, it follows that the date of the settlement of the primitive Vels in the south cannot be earlier than the eleventh century B.C. This date is not much later than the period of the Maha Bharata war, which is held, on the strength of many weighty reasons, to have occurred in the 12th [1] or the 13th [2] century B.C., by such sound scholars as the Hon. Mr. Romesh Chunder Dutt and Mr. Velandai Gopala Aiyar, B.A., besides others of no less research and culture. This remarkable propinquity of what is apparently the probable age of the colonization of parts of the south by the Vels to the epoch of the great Bharata war is noteworthy, as it fully corroborates the tradition that it was after the decease of Sri Krishna that the Velpula princes and people removed to the south.[3] To determine the date of this event within narrower limits than those above indicated is hardly possible without ampler data than those, at present, available to us.

I shall now briefly rehearse the story of how the sons of Velpulam and their chiefs emigrated to Dravida and founded powerful and prosperous colonies in that country in ancient times. Numerous bands of Yadavas quitting Velpulam, where they had been dwelling since they left their old home in the valley of the Ganges, moved down to the forest tracts in the south, cleared the forests, and created there a new home for themselves. Being a civilized race, they knew well the arts of peace as well as of war, including those of husbandry, weaving, making pottery, and the crafts of the five artificers, a knowledge of which was indispensable for a colonizing race like them. Long before these Yadava immigrants entered

---

[1] "Chronology of Ancient India."—*Vide* chapter on "The date of the Maha Bharata war."—V. J. T.

[2] Dutt's "Ancient India," p. 10.

[3] The "Maha Bharata" refers to a Pandya named Saranga Dwaja who fought on the side of the Pandavas in the great war, and according to Tamil books, the Chera and the Chola kings were also allied with the Pandavas in that war. As the Pandyas have always been allowed to be the oldest dynasty of Southern India or the Tamil country, it appears to be unlikely that the original founder of that royal house flourished at such a late date as that here advocated.—V. J. T.

the Tamil country,[1] a powerful and numerous race of people called "Nagas," and some other races which had descended into India from the north-east of "Aryavarta," were holding it, as permanent settlers, under their own kings. We learn from the old works (in Sanscrit) how, about the time of the Maha Bharata war, the above races had already spread out and formed permanent colonies in Tamilakam. As the learned Mr. Kanakasabhai Pillai has, in his valuable work, dealt with this subject so fully as to meet with the approbation of his readers, it will be superfluous for me to dwell on it further. It suffices to say that the above-mentioned Nagas, and other foreign settlers in Tamilakam, subdued the older inhabitants of the country, and imposed their own rule upon them. It was at this time, when the Naga and Mongolian supremacy was fully established in Dravida, that the Yadavas of Velpulam, clearing the great forests which covered the districts in the north of Dravida, and founding colonies in them under their own chiefs, gradually advanced further south [2] into the Tamil country. The districts which they thus cleared up, improved, and rendered fit for cultivation, they made their own by settling in them permanently under their own chiefs. Another section of these Yadavas, whose wealth consisted in

---

[1] According to Mr. Ḳanakasabhai Pillai "Villavar," *i.e.*, the bowmen, and "Minavar" (represented by the modern Minas) were the oldest inhabitants of the Tamil country, who, in course of time, were subdued by a numerous and powerful race called the Nagas, whose modern representatives are the Maravas, Kallar, Kurumbar, and Parathavar or Paravar. These were followed by races of Mongolian origin or extraction called "Yakshas" or "Yakkos" by the Sanscrit and Pali chroniclers, and identical with the Velala community of Southern India.—*Vide* "Tamils Eighteen Hundred Years Ago," chap. IV., p. 39.

[2] The gradual extension, here referred to, of political power from the north to the south of Tamilakam, by the Vels of the Maharatta country, receives no support from either the situation or the tradition of the origin of the Pandiyan kingdom. The earliest Tamil settlement, in so far as our present knowledge of it goes, lay, not on the northern border, as is here assumed, but in the southernmost section of Dravida, Mount Pothiyil near Cape Comorin being one of its most hallowed spots.—V. J. T.

The festival of Indra called "Indra Vilavu" would seem to have been one of the most popular festivals of the Tamils in ancient times. Indra was a peculiarly Indian god. The Maravas, who are admittedly

live stock, preferred a nomadic life with their flocks of sheep and cattle in the jungles and forests of the outlying portions of the country. Those of the Yadavas who adopted a settled life in the Nadus, or cultivated portions of the country, were called " Kilar," *i.e.*, " landlords," and " Velalas," from "Vel," the name of their mother country. These, living in societies, and prospering in the districts they made cultivable and fertile, gradually became experts in the various arts and crafts that were necessary for their material welfare, and attained to a mature civilization in process of time. The god whom these Aryan Kshatryas worshipped in order to ensure the blessings of fertility and prosperity of their land, was Indra, the rain god of the primitive Aryas. That the worship of Indra was an ancient practice of these people is proved by the references one meets with in the Puranic stories to the festivals of Indra celebrated by the Yadavas at Govardhana. As their more primitive abodes were in the districts about the Ganges, they called themselves " Gungaputras,"[1] *i.e.*, " the children of Gunga," and " Gungavamsas," *i.e.*, " the tribe of Gunga," or " those of the race of the Gunga," and the petty kings who ruled over them were called " Velir " and " Venmar."

Now, that section of the Yadavas who chose a nomadic life in the forests, tending their flocks of sheep and cattle, were

---

aborigines, claim to be the progeny of Indra, while their connection with the Pandiyas, who were known also as " Marar," was always of so intimate a kind that it seems hard to suppose the existence of any racial difference between them. The princes of the Maravas have, from ancient times, claimed kinship with the Cholas of the Solar race, and once the connection between these two races is allowed, the Indra festival celebrated in times of old in the Chola capital must, far from being an alien importation into the Tamil country, be looked upon as entirely indigenous, in its origin and development, to pre-Aryan India. It is worthy of notice that the late Professor Huxley considered the Maravas and the other South Indian races allied to them as kinsmen of the ancient Egyptians, whose kings bore the proud title of " the Sons of Ra," *i.e.*, the sun.—V. J. T.

[1] " Kankaikulaththar " is one of the names of the Tamil Velalas. Mr. Kanakasabhai Pillai identifies them with the "Gangaridæ " of ancient Greek writers.—*Vide* his " Tamils Eighteen Hundred Years Ago," p. 114.

on that account called "Ayar,"[1] "Kovalar," and "Mullai-nilamakkal" by the Tamil people. Immigrants from Velpulam as they also were, not being in contact with the civilized population of the Nadus, *i.e.*, the towns and villages of the country, they were not so well posted up in the practical arts and crafts of life, or so refined and cultured as the former, *i.e.*, the Yadavas inhabiting the towns and villages. Their tribal gods were Kannan, *i.e.*, Krishna, and Baladeva,[2] who, as Avatars of Tirumal, *i.e.*, the holy Vishnu, had incarnated in their race; and they celebrated frequent festivals and held dances in honour of these gods. According to the following passages in "Kalithogei," this shepherd race would appear to have accompanied the original founder of the Pandiyan family to the south, namely :—

(1) "The excellent clans of 'Ayar'[3] who came along with the illustrious house which 'Thennavan,'[4] whose virtue never fades, planted in olden times."

(2) "The great (shepherd) families who followed the imperishable house."

It has been pointed out (by eminent scholars) that Katyayana, who lived during the reign of king Nanda in the first half of the fourth century B.C., and who wrote "Varthikas" to explain the sutras of Panini, besides alluding to the Cholás and the Pandiyas (by name), refers,[5] indirectly, to the ancestry

[1] Mr. Kanakasabhai Pillai thinks that the "Ayar" are identical with the "Ahirs" of the Sanscrit Puranas.—*Vide* "Tamils Eighteen Hundred Years Ago," p. 57.

[2] Same as "Bala Raman."

[3] Mr. Kanakasabhai Pillai, as elsewhere noticed, identifies these "Ayar" races with the "Ahirs" or "Abirs" of the Sanscrit records. They were a non-Aryan people who inhabited, at first, the lower valley of the Indus, but in later times moved down to the south and occupied the regions about Guzerat. The fact that these shepherd races paid reverence to the "Jakshas" would seem to indicate some sort of ethnical affinity between them, the "Yakshas," and "Rakshasas" of ancient India.—*Vide* "Tamils Eighteen Hundred Years Ago," chap. XV., p. 229.

[4] "The King of the South," a name applied to the Pandiyas. "Thennan" is only another form of the same name, but it is sometimes interpreted as meaning "the lord of the coconut groves."—V. J. T.

[5] "Varthika on Panini," IV., 1-168.

of the latter by stating that one sprung from an individual of the tribes of the Pandus should be called a "Pandya."[1] The following facts have also been adduced (by learned men) as furnishing further material proofs of the descent of the Pandiyas from the Pandus, namely: they were said to have belonged, like the Pandus, to the Lunar race; their capital, Mathurai,[2] was named after one of the ancient capitals of the Lunar race in the north; and the Pandiyas called themselves "Panchavar,"[3] *i.e.*, the "descendants of the five," to indicate their common origin with the five sons of Pandu. The Tamil

---

[1] The name "Pandiyan" has also been explained as meaning "old," from "Pandu," from which it is held by many to have been derived. In the "Mahavansa," the first reference to the Pandiyan king is in the form of "king Pandava of Southern Mathura," and occurs in connection with the marriage of king Vijaya with the daughter of the Pandiya. The forms "Pandu" and "Pandi" are also to be found in the "Mahavansa" later on. There is, however, no reference in Tamil literature to "Pandu" of the Maha Bharata as a remote ancestor of the Pandavas. According to Dr. Oppert (*vide* his "Original Inhabitants of Bharata Varsha") Pandiyan is a contracted form of "Pallandiyan," *i.e.*, the lord of the Pallas, whom he identifies with the Pallavas, Ballas, Ballalas, and Velalas. Taking all the above views into consideration, the correct view would appear to be that the Pandiyas were a very ancient race of agriculturists related to the Pandæ or the Pandus of ancient India. It seems important to note that the agricultural class among the Telugus is still known as the "Panta," *i.e.*, the old race.—V. J. T.

[2] According to the "Ramayana," Uttarakandam, Northern or Uttara Mathura, was the capital of Madhu, a relative of Ravana, king of the Yakshas and Rakshasas of Lanka. His son Lavana was king of Mathura at the time of the Rama-Ravana war. It is worthy of notice that "Madhu" and "Yadu" are strictly synonymous terms—while "Yadu," the ancestor of the Yadavas, was, according to the Puranic legend, also the progenitor of the Rakshasas. The "Ayar," *i.e.*, the shepherd races of the Pandiyan kingdom, who claimed to have come down to the south with the ancestors of the Pandiyas, worshipped not only Krishna and Balarama of the Yadava race, but also the Yakshas who were the enemies of Rama. There seems to be no difficulty, therefore, in attributing the foundation of the Northern Mathura of the classics to a Yaksha dynasty with which the Pandiyas were connected.—V. J. T.

[3] Marco Polo says that the Pandiyan kingdom was, at the time of his visit, ruled over by five brother-princes of the Pandiyan race, and the same state of things is said to have prevailed when the sceptre of the Pandiyas finally passed into the hands of the Telugu conqueror. The

records declare that the Cholas[1] also, likewise claimed Muchukunta of the Solar race as their first great ancestor, and the Puranas say that this Muchukunta was a devotee, and one greatly favoured, of Sri Krishna. Leaving this aside, we learn from Tamil literature that the nomadic Yadavas who roamed about in the forests, had, at first, their own line of kings, which was exterminated by the Cholas[2] and the Cheras[3] in later times. The Yadava tribes who thus entered and settled in the Tamil country, Kshatriyas by rank as they were primitively, being, nevertheless, split up as time passed on into many separate communities, owing to differences of occupation that had developed during the long centuries of colonizing work upon which they had embarked without any intercourse with their Aryan kindred and compeers in social status, abandoned their primitive customs and habits little by little. They, nevertheless, never lost their hereditary valour and indomitable energy. The Velir tribes, who were thus forced by the stress of circumstances to take to such diverse callings as husbandry, the making of pottery, the five crafts, &c., generation after generation, were, in course of time, looked upon as separate and distinct communities, having no racial kinship with one another, so that the facts of their common ancestry and origin were entirely forgotten with the lapse of time. The caste of potters are, at present, known in the Tamil country as (குயவர்) "Kuyavar." They were, however, not known by

---

"Mahavansa" also refers in one place to the five brothers who ruled over the kingdom of Mathurai (*vide* chapter XC., vv. 43 and 44). The name "Panchavan" applied to the Pandiyan king in Tamil literature may, therefore, be explained as containing nothing more than a reference to this historical fact.—V. J. T.

[1] The "Koli" race of Maharashtra has always laid claim to be the descendants of the Solar race through Yuvanashwa and Mandata. But this race is held to be aboriginal, and therefore non-Aryan; the resemblance between "Koli" and "Choli" is, however, striking, especially when it is contemplated along with the fact that Uraiyur, the capital of the Cholas, was known also as "Koli-ur," *i.e.*, the city of Koli.—V. J. T.

[2] "Pattinapalai," line 288.

[3] "Pathittupaththu," 71, 88.

this name in ancient times. A study of Tamil literature would disclose the fact that their more ancient name is (வேட்கோ) "Ved-Ko," which signifies, apparently, "that they were descended from the race of Velpula kings." We also find the name "Irun Ko Vel" used for the potters in the old classics, which, however, appears to be only a derivative metathetically obtained from the former. The passage "Nanmathi Vedkochchirar" (நன்மதிவேட்கோச்சிறார்), *i.e.*, "the little ones of the Vedkos possessing good sense and intelligence," occurs in an ode in "Purrananooru,"[1] and it obviously implies a certain amount of culture and refinement among these potters in former times. Even to-day the potters adhere to the "Anuddanam" of the Aryas, and unlike others who were of the Vel community, but have abandoned their national customs and practices, are still in the habit of wearing the sacred thread of the Dwijas or the twice-born. Furthermore, "Velar" (வேளார்) is in use among them as an honorary title even at the present day.

The above facts furnish us with an amount of cumulative evidence which appears to me to be sufficient—and so too it indeed must to every sober and unprejudiced mind—to establish beyond doubt that the class of potters known as Vedkovar (வேட்கோவர்) to pundits of old Tamil literature, were originally inhabitants of Velpulam, and that they formed an integral part of the Velir race of ancient Tamilakam.

The story preserved in the commentary on "Tolkappiam" that the poet Nakkirar, incensed at the audacity of a potter named "Vedkokkuyakkodan," who had ventured to extol the beauties of Ariyam[2] and to speak disparagingly of Tamil, cursed and killed him with an imprecatory ode, would seem to point to the existence of Sanscrit culture among these Vedkovar in ancient times.

Of all these Yadava tribes, the most numerous, prosperous, and powerful one was the tribe of Velir, who made their living by means of the plough. The learned Nachchar in his

---

[1] *Vide* ode 32.

[2] Sanscrit.

commentary on "Tolkappiam" writes about them as follows, namely:—

"The Velalas[1] consist of two classes, namely, 'Uluthuviththunpor' (*i.e.*, those who get their fields ploughed by others, or in other words, who possess the means to employ labour in the cultivation of their fields), and 'Uluthunpor' (*i.e.*, those who ploughed their fields themselves, or those who are not rich enough to employ labour in ploughing, &c., their fields). Of these, the former, *i.e.*, Uluthuviththunpor, belonged originally to Pidavur, Alundur, Nangur, Navur, Alancheri, Perunchikkal, Vallam, Kilar, and other cities of the Chola country, and were employed by the reigning monarchs as governors of provinces and districts, and commanders of their armies; and they were entitled to high privileges, being known as 'Vel' and 'Arasu,' and honoured with the title of 'Kavithi' in the Pandiyan country, and being born ot the families of the petty kings and nobles, they had the privilege of giving their daughters in marriage to the paramount rulers of the country." Moreover, "invading the enemy's country, repelling attacks made on their own country by the enemy, and acting as peace envoys, were amongst the privileges of the Velalas." And further, in his comments on another sutra of "Tolkappiam," he ascribes the following six duties to the Velalas, namely, "teaching, giving, ploughing, tending cattle, engaging in trade, and loyalty to the king." It may be observed that tending cattle and engaging in commerce are here included amongst the six duties of the Velalas. The facts above noticed make

---

1 "The Tamils are, like the Romans of old, a nation of yeomen," and like them, hold agriculture in the highest esteem. "The world wheels behind the plough, says the Tamil sage Tiruvalluvar," of all work, therefore, "ploughing is the chief." The Portuguese historian of India, F. Sousa, writing of the social divisions of his time (17th century), says: "The most renowned families are the Rajahs, an ingenious people, who would rather lose their lives than their arms in battle, and the Brahmans, who contend with the Rajahs for precedence. The Chetties are the richest merchants. The Vellalar or the country people are held in such esteem that kings marry their daughters to them."—*Vide* "Report on Ceylon Census, 1901," by P. Arunachalam, M.A., C.C.S., vol. I., p. 197, paras. 47 and 49.—V. J. T.

it fully clear, it must be admitted that the great Tamil monarchs of old not only held many of the Velalas in very great esteem and regard and employed them in high offices of State under them, but honoured them to such extent as to accept in marriage the daughters of the more powerful among them—not a few of whom held the position of petty kings over large districts. Many instances of such marriages (of the supreme kings of Tamilakam with the daughters of their Vel feudatories) are mentioned in "Pathittupaththu" and other ancient Tamil works. We conclude, therefore, that it was because these Velir, who were a section of the primitive Aryas, had attained an extreme degree of maturity in the civilization and refinement of the time, that the great Tamil potentates, who were of high descent, treated them as their equals in social rank, and considered it not beneath them to intermarry with their families. It is to this fact that Tolkappian also refers in his sutra 79 of the section on "Puraththinai Iyal."

Moreover, we gather from the Tamil records that, when the Vels first set out on the enterprise of founding small kingdoms for themselves, they came into frequent collisions with the three Tamil kings, and that Konkanam, Muththoor [1] Koottam, Pothigai Nadu, Milalaik Kootam [2] Kunrur, &c., were amongst their oldest settlements in the south. In subsequent times, however, the paramount rulers [3] of Tamilakam

---

[1] Muththoor Koottam is also called Muththoortukkoottam. This was one of the districts of the Chola country which was, at one time, conquered by the Pandiyan king and annexed to his kingdom. It is supposed to be now represented by the districts lying round the modern "Muththu Peddai."

[2] This is situated in the Pandiyan country, and it may be remarked that one of its divisions is even now called "Dwarapati Nadu."

[3] That the Pandiyas were Velalas by race receives strong support from the traditional account of their origin elsewhere quoted as preserved by Nachchar, namely, that they were of the family of Sri Krishna of Dwarakai of the Yadava race. Says the learned author of the last Ceylon Census Report: "When the Tamils are spoken of in South India, the Velalas are meant, as being the Tamils *par excellence*, both the Brahmans at the top of the modern social system and the aborigines at the bottom being excluded. This seems to indicate that these two are regarded as heterogeneous elements not reduced to the

who became connected with their families by marriage, took them and their small kingdoms under their own protection, treated with very great regard and esteem many of the cultured and civilized Velala nobles who were the kinsmen of these Vel princes, and beside conferring on them marks of honour and distinction and liberal grants of lands, prized their services so highly as to appoint them their chief ministers and military commanders. It is said in "Chilappathikaram" that one of the most distinguished ministers of the Chera king "Chenkudduvan" was "Alumpil Vel," who was one of the petty kings of the time. The Velala nobles who held the position of chief ministers under the Pandiyas were honoured with the title of "Kavithi," while those who were so employed under the Cholas bore the high title of "Enathi,"[1] as can be seen from the passage "looking at the face of the Choliya Enathi" which occurs in "Manimekali."[2] The fact that Karikal Chola honoured these Vels above all his other subjects, and took them under his special patronage, granting them the over-lordship of twenty-four Kottams consisting of seventy-four Nadus, is proved by extant sannas and writings.

According to "Tolkappiam,"[3] which was composed in the latter part of what historical experts have designated "the

---

national type. * * * In this race of farmers (*i.e.*, the Velalas) three families appear to have early attained to a predominant position, and they founded the famous Pandya, Chola, and Chera dynasties."—*Vide* "The Ceylon Census Report, 1901," p. 196, paras. 46 and 47. The author of "The Tamils Eighteen Hundred Years Ago" has asserted the same thing of the Tamil dynasties. He says: "The three Tamil tribes Maranmar, Thirayar, and Vanavar founded respectively the Tamil kingdoms subsequently known as the Pandya, Chola, and Chera kingdoms. The Chera, Chola, and Pandya kings and most of the petty chiefs of Tamilakam belonged to the tribe of Velalas."—*Vide* pp. 50 and 113.—V. J. T.

[1] This title was not confined to any particular class of the Tamils. Enathi Nayanar, one of the Sivite saints, was a distinguished scion of the Shantara or toddy-drawing race.—V. J. T.

[2] One of the Buddhist epics now extant.—V. J. T.

[3] Tolkappian, the author of "Tolkappiam," was, according to the traditionary accounts preserved in Tamil works whose classical value has never been questioned, a disciple of Agastiyar, and it is not, therefore, clear how his date can be brought down to such a late period as the 3rd century B.C.—V. J. T.

sutra period of Sanskrit literature," tilling the ground was the only means of livelihood adopted by the Velalas, "and they had no other." This statement means, it appears to me, nothing more than that agriculture was the chief occupation of the greater portion of them. For none will deny that there were among them many who, as distinguished chiefs owning small kingdoms, exercised duties appropriate only to the royalty, while there were also others who served the Tamil kings in high offices of state, and were counted worthy of high royal favours and marks of honour, as the following quotations from "Tolkappiam" should unmistakably show:—

(1) "The rights and privileges natural to the royalty belong to others also besides the king."

(2) "The bow, the lance, the feet-rings, the kanni (*i.e.*, the bouquet), the garland, the necklace, the chariot, and the sword belong to others also of ancient ancestry besides the king."

(3) "The feet-ring and the kanni are the substantial awards they receive in the service of the king."

We understand from the above passages, of which the first two enumerate the privileges of the Velir and the last one those of the Velalas, that most of the distinctions or privileges which were held appropriate only to crowned heads belonged to the Velir too, while to the Velalas belonged the privileges of wearing only the feet-ring and the kanni. As the social customs and occupations of the Velir were, in the time of the grammarian Tolkappian, identical, not with those peculiar to either the Kshatriyas or the Vaisyas taken separately, but with those of both these classes taken together, that grammarian naturally ascribed to them duties belonging to both, *i.e.*, the Kshatriyas and the Vaisyas. But the commentator, where the text appeared to him to imply a high social standing for the Velalas, there invariably ascribes a noble and high descent to them, and where the status implied by the text is an inferior one, there he uniformly assigns it to the "Uluthunpor," or the poorer class among the Velalas. This, of course, represents their condition then. Further, as the greater number of those who formed the higher aristocracy of ancient Tamilakam belonged to the Velir class, the term Velir, gradually losing its primitive signification, came to be used and taught in the Tamil lexicons, in later times, as a synonym for "a petty king," irrespective of race or tribe. But as we do not find it to be so employed in ancient Tamil works, it is obviously an erroneous usage of a subsequent period. And further, as the Velalas, who were the kith and kin of the Velir, adopted agriculture as their special occupation from generation to generation more than any other community of the land, that occupation was, by and by, called by a designation derived from their name. I refer above to the word "Velanmai,"[1] which literally means "the occupation of the Vels," *i.e.*, agriculture. Moreover, from the extreme regard in which the Vels were held on account of their unbounded and hereditary munificence, their strict integrity and faith, as well as their hereditary right to minor kingships, the word Vel came to signify, in course of time, respectively "a benefactor," "truthfulness,"[2] and "an Ilavarasu," *i.e.*, an heir-apparent to the throne. It may, in this connection, be observed that even now the ancient name of Velir is very commonly met with among certain classes of Velalas residing at Therkaddur in the Native State of Puducottai in South India.

To recapitulate now the results of our inquiry so far into the origin of the Velir race. By the tradition existing in South India that the primitive Velir were immigrants from Dwaraka, and of the line of Kannan,[3] a tradition materially supported by a passage in "Purrananooru," a work of high antiquity, the Velir become identified as Yadavas by race. With regard to the Yadavas, their emigration to the south and the establishment of permanent colonies of them there, are supported, not only by clear, though indirect, references

---

[1] "Vellalar" is also said to be a contracted form of "Vella-Alar," meaning "the lords of the 'Vellam,'" *i.e.*, flood. In this sense it means substantially the same as "Karalar," *i.e.*, the lords of the rain, which is another name by which the Tamil agriculturists are known. — V. J. T.

[2] Some derive "Vel," in the sense of truthfulness, from the root "Vel," meaning "white."—V. J. T.

[3] The same as Krishna.

thereto in ancient Indian literature, but also by a tradition existing in the north of India much to the same effect. Furthermore, that the Velir were Yadavas by race is made evident from the agreement, in many respects, between them and the Hoysalas, who came down from Dwaraka and ruled in the south in later times. The terms Velir and Velalas, by which they were known, appertained to them in consequence of their having come from Velpulam, which was the name of their mother-country. The appellation Vel, moreover, is found used for a line of kings of ancient Deccan, namely, the Chalukkyas, and as these Chalukkyas themselves belonged to the same Yadava race, the identity of race of these two communities, the Velir of the Tamil country and the Chalukkya rulers, seems to be well established. Moreover, the legend of the birth of a first ancestor from the sacred pot of an ascetic which is common to both of them would seem to carry this identification almost to perfection. Again, the identification of the Chalukkyas, the Yadava Narapatis of Vijayanagara, and the Vels of Tamilakam with the ancient race of Andhras who ruled over Magadha, is remarkably confirmatory of the same conclusion. The country of Ven, which was one of the twelve of Kodun Tamil Nadus, was identical with the primitive country of the Yadavas, and it agrees with other facts that the time of the emigration of the primitive Vels to the Tamil country was about the eleventh century B.C. The above is most probably the correct story of the colonization of large districts of the south by the Yadava race.

To conclude, then: the Velir families who, as stated in the preceding pages, emigrated from Velpulam and settled as rulers in several parts of the south, and the great community of the Velalas who were their followers and kinsmen have, by their lavish munificence, by the titles and privileges which they were deemed worthy to receive at the hands of the kings, by their benevolence to the poor and the helpless, and last, but not least, by their invincible valour and strength that never stooped to oppress, earned, from ages past, the highest degree of fame and reputation for themselves throughout the Tamil country. Not one of the great Tamil poets of earlier or later periods, who went to their mansions and sang their praises, ever came back thence unbenefited or unrewarded. There is, indeed, no nook or corner in all Tamilakam where the open-handed liberality of the primitive Velir is remembered except with feelings of praise and admiration. Of this type were the great Vallals Vel Avi, Vel Ay, Vel Evvi, Vel Pari, and Vel Pekan, who all flourished about 1,800 years ago, and whose beautiful histories, too long to be here inserted, may well form the subject of a future essay. Not less illustrious and great were also their distinguished descendants, in sounding whose praises the poets of a later date have exhausted all their command of language as well as the resources of poesy.

"Tho' things diverse from diverse sages' lips we learn,
'Tis wisdom's part in each the true thing to discern."—

Pope's translation of Tiruvalluvar's "Kural," stanza 423.